Drama for Students, Volume 30

Project Editor: Sara Constantakis Rights Acquisition and Management: Robyn Young Composition: Evi Abou-El-Seoud Manufacturing: Rhonda Dover

Imaging: John Watkins

Product Design: Pamela A. E. Galbreath, Jennifer Wahi Digital Content Production: Allie Semperger Product Manager: Meggin Condino © 2013 Gale, Cengage Learning

ALL RIGHTS RESERVED. No part of this work covered by the copyright herein may be reproduced, transmitted, stored, or used in any form or by any means graphic, electronic, or mechanical, including but not limited to photocopying, recording, scanning, digitizing, taping, Web distribution, information networks, or information storage and retrieval systems, except as permitted under Section 107 or 108 of the 1976 United States Copyright Act, without the prior written permission of the publisher.

Since this page cannot legibly accommodate all copyright notices, the acknowledgments constitute an extension of the copyright notice.

For product information and technology assistance, contact us at **Gale Customer Support, 1-800-877-4253.**

For permission to use material from this text or product, submit all requests online at www.cengage.com/permissions.

Further permissions questions can be emailed to **permissionrequest@cengage.com** While every effort has been made to ensure the reliability of the information presented in this publication, Gale, a part of Cengage Learning, does not guarantee the accuracy of the data contained herein. Gale accepts no payment for listing; and inclusion in the publication of any organization, agency, institution, publication, service, or individual does not imply endorsement of the editors or publisher. Errors brought to the attention of the publisher and verified to the satisfaction of the publisher will be corrected in future editions.

Gale
27500 Drake Rd.
Farmington Hills, MI, 48331-3535

ISBN-13: 978-0-7876-9640-5
ISBN-10: 0-7876-9640-4
ISSN 1094-9232

This title is also available as an e-book.

ISBN-13: 978-1-4144-4942-5
ISBN-10: 1-4144-4942-9
Contact your Gale, a part of Cengage Learning sales representative for ordering information.

Printed in Mexico
1 2 3 4 5 6 7 17 16 15 14 13

Far Away

Caryl Churchill 2000

Introduction

Caryl Churchill is generally regarded as among the greatest of living playwrights. Her body of work represents a hard-line socialist critique of British society. *Far Away* uses the apocalyptic roots of Marxism and presents political ideas in what can nearly be described as a religious allegory. Churchill draws heavily on the European tradition of leftist theater, and *Far Away* is heavily influenced by the surrealists' "theater of cruelty" and the epic theater of Bertolt Brecht. Churchill feels she can no longer directly convey her political analysis and so turns to a style thick with symbols, creating a dramatic world in which the power of language itself fails.

Author Biography

Churchill was born in London, England, on September 3, 1938. Her family moved to Montreal, in Canada, ten years later, but she returned to England to attend Oxford University beginning in 1957. Churchill says that while she wrote enthusiastically since childhood, at Oxford she began to specialize in drama and had her plays (such as *Downstairs* and *Having a Wonderful Time*, neither of which has been published) performed by college drama societies. In 1960, she published an article in *The Twentieth Century* praising the work of the Royal Court Theatre, which had been founded in 1956 to produce avant garde (experimental) theater. She would go on to develop a close relationship with the Royal Court, which has been responsible for the premieres of most of her plays, including *Far Away* (2000). In 1961, Churchill was introduced by a mutual friend to the prominent literary agent Peggy Ramsay, who worked to establish Churchill's career. After graduation, Churchill married the barrister (a type of attorney) David Harter, with whom she had three children. She began to write brief radio plays, beginning with *The Ants* (also unpublished), which premiered on the British Broadcasting Corporation (BBC) radio in 1962. Throughout the 1960s, Churchill continued to write more radio plays that were generally directed on the air by John Tydeman. She also worked on stage dramas, but she did not have her breakthrough on the stage until 1972, when the Royal Court Theatre put on her *Owners*. By 1974, she was the resident writer at the Royal Court, where Tydeman has became a leading director.

Churchill is unusually reclusive for a modern author and does not give interviews with the press or speak out in the usual academic and critical venues to explain her work. The main theme of Churchill's plays is social justice. Her husband too has gradually given up a more standard law practice and works as an advocate for the poor and oppressed. Among her best regarded plays, *Top Girls* (1982) addresses the compromises and choices that the new roles offered by feminism place on women, and *Serious Money* (1987) deals with the problem of greed in the financial industry. *Blue Heart* (1997) is about the limitations that language imposes on drama. *Far Away* was staged as a successful production in 2000 at the Royal Court Theatre, directed by Stephen Daldry, and has been revived since then all over the world.

In 2009, Churchill's *Seven Jewish Children*, a ten-minute play criticizing Israeli attitudes toward Palestinians, premiered at the Royal Court, and it has brought her even greater fame. It plays on the irony of a nation that was founded in reaction to the Holocaust oppressing a minority. She encourages it to be produced by letting it be performed without royalties so long as the proceeds are donated to charities for Palestinians. It has been more widely performed than any of her other works. Although she has won a number of awards for her plays (including the Susan Smith Blackburn Prize in 1983 and 1987 and the *Evening Standard* Prize, also in 1987), they are too experimental in nature for her to have been in the running for mainstream awards such as the Tony or the Pulitzer.

Plot Summary

According to Philip Roberts in his book *About Churchill*, the playwright "increasingly in her work delivers her text to those she trusts to create it in performance." As a practical matter, this seems to mean that there is considerable variance between the published form of her work and the productions in which she is personally involved. What has been left out of the published texts can sometimes be reconstructed from the comments of Roberts and other critics who viewed the original production. In other cases, the difference are tantalizingly vague. For instance, Roberts says that there are four speaking roles in the play, though there are only three in the printed text. The printed text contains virtually no stage directions or descriptions, since Churchill feels those creative decisions should be left to the director, crew, and actors of the play.

Far Away is divided into three acts, indicated simply by boldfaced numbers in the script. The second act is divided into six scenes. As the initial production begins, the curtain is down, showing a painting of the English countryside. When the curtain rises, Harper is singing the hymn "There Is a Happy Land Far, Far Away," which refers to the Christian idea of heaven. This is evidently the inspiration for the play's title.

Act 1

The first scene takes place in the bedroom of Harper, the aunt of Joan, the main character of the play. When the play is performed, Joan has been presented as a small child in this scene, played by a different actress than in the later acts.

Joan is visiting her aunt Harper, who lives in the country. One night at 2:00 a.m., long after her bedtime, the little girl goes into her aunt's room and complains that she cannot sleep. Harper suggests all sorts of reasons this might be, such as sleeping for the first night in a strange bed or missing her pet. But it is none of those. Joan finally admits that she is cold, and Harper, ignoring possible metaphorical meanings of the term, takes her statement at face value; she offers to solve the problem with more blankets. But the issue is not really resolved, and the aunt continues questioning the child. Harper reveals that she had gone outside—not through the front door but through her window onto the roof. Harper is naturally upset to hear this, because there is some risk of falling in that case. But Joan turns the conversation toward how much brighter the stars seem in the country than in the city. As slowly as possible, Joan lets Harper drag out of her what actually happened.

Joan went out through her window because she heard a noise: someone screaming. Hiding in the tree by the house, Joan saw her uncle (Harper's husband, who does not appear as a character in the play) pushing someone into a shed. There were many people inside the shed crying. Joan could hear them because she climbed down from the tree and listened with her ear against the wall. She also noticed a great deal of blood on the ground. Harper denies this, but Joan says, "I slipped in it." Harper claims it must have come from a dog that had been run over earlier in the day.

Joan does not press the point any further, but she asks why there were children in the shed. The light in the shed was on, and she could see that there were children in there, some of whose faces were covered in blood.

Now Harper acknowledges that there was something secret going on in the shed and tells Joan what is going on. She insists that Joan's uncle is helping the children and adults in the shed to escape. Harper doesn't go into unnecessary detail, as one might not to a child, but the audience is led to believe that these people are under threat from some kind of tyrannical government. If Joan ever reveals the secret she'll be in danger too. Harper suggests that Joan's uncle is doing something along the lines of hiding Jews in Nazi-occupied Europe and smuggling them to safety. Harper now admits that what she had said before (suggesting the injured dog, for example, to explain the blood) was a lie, to keep the secret. She assures Joan: "I'm trusting you with the truth now. You must never talk about it or you'll put your uncle's life in danger and mine and even your own. You won't even say anything to your parents."

But this isn't everything Joan saw. She saw her uncle beating a man and a child. Harper explains that this was a traitor who had infiltrated their rescue operation. The child was the traitor's son. Harper reassures Joan that now she is a hero for helping to keep the secret. In the morning she can do more by helping her aunt to clean up the blood.

Act 2

It is now several years later; the setting is a hat maker's shop. Each scene in act 2 takes place one day after the previous scene.

ACT 2, SCENE 1

Joan, now an adult, is sitting at a work bench with Todd, and they are both making hats. There is a good deal of incidental conversation about the work that they are doing, but again a hint is given that provides background for the audience and moves the plot along. Joan has just finished a university degree in millinery, or hat making. Joan understood that she has been hired by the most prestigious hat workshop, but Todd lets her know that there are many things wrong with the place. Work rules are always being changed to make matters more difficult and reduce their pay. He sounds her out about some kind of joint action to oppose the management.

ACT 2, SCENE 2

Churchill has made a point in the play of writing lines that are much more like real conversation than dramatic dialogue. Action often begins and ends in the middle of conversations without context. But at the beginning of this scene, as Joan and Todd continue to work the next day, that begins to break down. The dialogue is literally incomprehensible:

Joan: Your turn.

Todd: I go for a swim in the river before work.

Joan: Isn't it dangerous?

Todd: Your turn.

Joan: I've got a pilot's license.

The *your turns* could mean they're taking turns using some hat making equipment; only the director could establish that by what he has the actors do on stage. If, on the other hand, the two are playing some kind of game where they reveal something unexpected about themselves in turn, that would actually provide some kind of context for Joan's "I've got a pilot's license," which does not seem to follow logically from Todd's earlier statement. Another possibility is that the conversation is being picked up in the middle, so there is no way to follow it. But the logical breakdown of the dialogue that begins here worsens throughout the play until words have no meaning left.

Todd mentions that he stays up late at night watching the trials on television. So far the audience has no way of understanding what that means. Todd also expresses concerns that the business practices of the workshop's executives are corrupt. He also starts courting Joan.

ACT 2, SCENE 3

This scene revisits the content of the previous one. Joan and Todd grow closer, and Todd complains about the management. The point is to model the repetitions that fill everyday life. It develops that the increasingly ridiculous hats they are making will be worn in a parade.

ACT 2, SCENE 4

Todd tells Joan he is going to confront their boss about improving work conditions. Besides what he considers the rightness of his cause, he is prepared to use blackmail. Todd knows certain details about improprieties in the workshop's finances and a journalist who might be interested. If he loses his job over it, Todd says, the only thing he would miss is Joan.

ACT 2, SCENE 5

The scene shifts to a parade of prisoners on their way to execution. They are wearing the hats that Todd and Joan made, and other hats that are equally ridiculous.

ACT 2, SCENE 6

Joan has won an award for one of the hats she made for the last parade. It will be preserved in the worship museum. In general, however, the hats are burned together with the bodies of the prisoners. Todd and Joan are clearly more concerned about the hats than the people.

Joan is beginning to return Todd's affection. While before she was indifferent to his concerns about their wages and work rules, she now flatters him by saying she feels inspired by his political and economic consciousness. Todd speaks briefly about what happened at the meeting he had the previous day. This was exactly nothing, but he imagines he must be on the verge of improving their situation. Joan volunteers that if Todd is fired, she will quit too.

Act 3

Several years later, Todd is hiding out at Harper's house. Joan is asleep in a bedroom upstairs. Todd and Harper talk about how animals are starting to kill people. They are taking sides with the various nations who are all fighting each other, the cats with the French and the ants with the Moroccans. The dialogue becomes more and more chaotic and meaningless, just random phrases snatched out of thin air. Todd has been fighting in the war, taking a sadistic pleasure in massacring children and animals. Joan comes downstairs and delivers a long final speech about her own perilous journey to reach the house, during which she may or may not have been attacked not just by animals, but by a river.

Characters

Harper

Harper is Joan's aunt with whom she is, in all probability, spending part of her summer vacation from school as a young child. Joan comes to her aunt because she is overwhelmed, having just seen her uncle brutalize and evidently murder at least some of a group of people he has locked in his garden shed. The girl is unable to say clearly what she has seen, but she wants her aunt to make the experience go away; she is unable to deal with it. The coldness that Joan complains of is emotional numbness. She slowly tells her story, recalling what she did and what she saw one step at a time.

Harper knows exactly what has been going on that night, but she responds to each segment of her niece's story as if it were the end, and that stage was all the girl witnessed. She does this because she desperately wants her niece not to know anything that has happened. At each new detail that Joan reveals, Harper provides an explanation that makes the thing witnessed seem innocent, but which is a lie. When Joan says she saw her uncle on the lawn, Harper tells her he was out for a walk. When Joan reveals that she saw him forcing someone to go into a shed, either a woman or a young man, the audience may well think the uncle was committing some kind of sexual assault, but Harper responds:

"Well I have to tell you, when you've been married as long as I have. There are things people get up to, it's natural, it's nothing bad, that's just friends of his your uncle was having a little party with." Whatever Harper means by this, the audience will think the uncle was involved in something that one would not want to discuss with a little girl and suspect that is what Harper was trying to cover up. She is constantly trying to persuade Joan with a false story that seems to explain the facts so far but without giving anything else away. But then Joan says she stepped in a pool of blood. Harper invents a dog run over by a truck, even supplying a made-up name and description of the animal. Finally, when Joan says that she saw her uncle torturing and murdering people, even children, Harper admits that everything she has said before is a lie, but she offers a new explanation that makes her husband out a hero. Supposedly he is helping innocent people escape the forces of oppression, and the people he killed were traitors. She had had to lie to protect Joan from knowing the dangerous truth. Young as she is, even Joan can see the improbability in this; she quite sensibly asks: "Why did you have me to stay if you've got this secret going on?" Harper has an answer for this too: while they help ferry truckloads of these people to safety periodically, the truck that came that night was unexpected. Joan finally accepts this as the truth.

But the audience may not be so reassured. Since Harper was lying about everything else, explaining everything away to her own advantage, why should this last story be any different? Doesn't it seem probable that the uncle is an agent of the forces of oppression, and he is torturing, terrorizing, and murdering because his purpose is to torture, terrorize, and murder? Other government agents and secret police in the history of the twentieth century also had families to whom they pretended to be virtuous heroes while they were really cowardly murders. People who live under totalitarianism (a system in which the government holds great power over every aspect of citizens' lives) to a surprising degree accept and internalize the propaganda of the state. They learn to explain away the horrors they witness every day by the kind of reasoning and fictions that Harper uses to persuade Joan. Harper is a symbol of the education and acceptance of falsehood that repression depends upon. Churchill's point in bringing this "education" into a home environment is to invite the audience to consider whether they might not have been re-educated in this way without realizing it.

Joan

Joan is the central character of the play, as well as a vehicle for Churchill to deliver her political message to the audience. *Far Away* is the story of Joan's growth and gaining of self-awareness. It is vital therefore to see the three acts of the play as corresponding to the three stages of Joan's life: childhood, physical maturity, and intellectual or spiritual maturity. The basis of Joan's characterization comes from her being portrayed at three different ages. In the first act, she is a small child who still sleeps with a stuffed animal. In the second act, she is a new graduate who is on her first day of the job. In the last act she is a mature adult, not necessarily many years older than in the second act, but with a completely altered perspective. This is clear in productions of the play, where Joan is generally played by two different actresses, a child in the first act and an adult in the other two, although Churchill stays as silent about this in the printed text as she does other details of staging.

One way to read the play is as the process of Joan's education. In the first act, she is taught to ignore or explain away the alarming facts about the world around her, and in the second she has learned her lesson and is oblivious to the atrocities she is witness to and even a participant in. In the third act, she throws off her childhood lessons and begins to be aware. As a result, the world she sees seems threatening and insane. Joan stands in for the audience. Churchill is using a very thin veil of fiction to tell the viewers that their life histories have been the same as Joan's. They were conditioned as children to ignore the forces of oppression and violence that are present in modern Western society, and continue to ignore their own share of the blame. She is calling on her audience to wake up and see the world in the same way that she does.

The Parade

Churchill lists the parade as a collective

character in the *dramatis personae* (a list of the characters given at the beginning of the script). The individuals making up the parade appear in only one scene, completely detached from the rest of the action of the play. Whereas the rest of the play takes place either in Harper's bedroom or the hat workshop, the parade must take place in some unspecified prison yard or place of public execution. The scene, without dialogue, is described only in the briefest terms in the text of the play: "A procession of ragged, beaten, chained prisoners, each wearing a hat, on their way to execution. The finished hats are even more enormous and preposterous than in the previous scene." Churchill also specifies the number of actors in the parade in the dramatis personae: "five is too few and twenty better than ten. A hundred?" Her point is for there to be an overwhelming number of people in this parade. In some productions, the parade is acted in deathly silence; in others, there is an emotive musical score.

The parade's members are wearing the hats that were being made by Joan and Todd. This comes as a shocking surprise. During the earlier part of the second act, it would be natural to assume that the hats were to be worn during some sort of happy, festive parade such as that held at Mardi Gras, not a public execution. But the prisoners are made to wear the hats as a strategy to dehumanize and humiliate them, to distract the members of the public who are watching them. Roberts comments in *About Churchill*, "Nothing demonstrates the utter contempt the prisoners are held in [more than] that they are fodder for millinery."

The dialogue between Joan and Todd makes it clear that the execution that will happen after the parade will be watched on national television by a large audience. Furthermore, while discussing Joan's prize-winning hat after the parade, they make it clear that the prisoners are burned along with the hats. The audience is left wondering if the prisoners might be burned alive, although no such brutal details are spelled out.

Todd

In the second act, Todd functions as the love interest for Joan, in what might be called a satire of a love story. His role in the third act, like Harper's in the first act, is simply to provide explanation about a world at war with itself, and that scene does nothing to build his character. In the second act, Todd complains about the working conditions at the hat workshop and engages in vaguely described political maneuverings to try and improve them. He thinks he has succeeded, but he seems too unsophisticated to realize that his employers have given him only meaningless bureaucrat-speak ("these things must be thought about") that means nothing will change. This is usually taken by scholars as Churchill's criticism of the failure of the British trade union movement as an instrument of socialist reform.

Themes

Apocalypse

The Greek word *apocalypse* means the bringing to light of something that has been hidden away. Often translated as *revelation*, apocalypse is the name given to a genre of literature that emerged in Judaism about the third century BCE and which was later taken up by early Christian writers. The subject matter of an apocalypse is the revelation of secrets about the universe given to the author by an angel or other divine agent. In the earliest apocalypse, the First Book of Enoch, the author is a given a tour of the universe. The Revelation of St. John, at the end of the New Testament, records visions of the future, specifically the end of the world in devastating war and natural disasters.

Topics for Further Study

- There are many videos posted at various places on the Internet that cut together stock footage in order to create a film trailer. As if you were mounting a production of *Far Away*, edit your own trailer for the play and post it to the Internet. Gather stock and other footage that may itself be unrelated to the play but whose images, edited together, suggest the themes of the play. Examples can be found online: for instance, one that was done for a student exercise (http://www.youtube.com/watch?v=czqFJaVmZxk) and one done for a professional stage production (http://www.youtube.com/watch?v=sCcgwuE0EJ8).

- Elin Diamond has suggested, without fully developing the idea, that *Far Away* presents a view of the world that is exactly opposite that given in an ancient Greek work, Seneca's *Thyestes* (which Churchill has translated). Read that play and write a paper comparing the two works, particularly paying attention to their views of the role of power in society.

- "Exquisite Corpse" is a game

invented by the surrealists to demonstrate the creative power of the human unconscious. It is meant to produce writing that on the surface makes no sense but that is capable of provoking a deeper meaning within the reader. The gradual breakdown of ordinary sense in the dialogue throughout *Far Away* is deeply indebted to this surrealist view of language. Organize a few rounds of this game among your classmates, splitting them into groups of five or six. To play, the group leader writes out on a sheet of paper a column of the names of the parts of speech in an order that makes a sentence, like so: article_____noun_____ The paper is handed around to each member of the group a who writes down an actual word of the indicated kind on the line, then folds the paper so the next player cannot see what was written before and passes it on, until the sentence is complete. The leader then reads what was written, makes any necessary adjustments for agreements of number or case, and reads out the randomly created sentence. The title of the game is itself a striking phrase created by this kind of random generation that

> would be unlikely to have been made up on purpose.

- The surrealist tone of *Far Away* would make it ideal for a graphic adaptation. For comparison, Shaun Tan's 2006 *The Arrival* is a graphic novel for young adults that uses surrealist imagery to deal with the theme of immigration. Make your own graphic novel based on an act or scene from *Far Away*.

The point of the genre is to show its readers that the world is fundamentally different than is usually assumed and that a changed way of living is called for as a consequence. This makes the apocalyptic genre very suitable for Churchill's purposes, since in *Far Away* she calls into question the common assumptions that the modern world is a place of freedom and justice. Churchill uses, as a model, the apocalypse that is described in Revelation. *Far Away* ends in a catastrophic global war in which all the nations of the earth fight against each other. Animals join in, with each species fighting for or against one side or another, and finally nature itself rises up against humanity. This is all described in the third act of *Far Away*, which begins with Todd and Harper discussing which nations and animals are to be trusted and describing attacks against people by deer and house cats. The climax of the play comes in Joan's narration of her trip to Harper's house:

> I could hardly walk but I got down to the river. There was a camp of Chilean soldiers upstream but they hadn't seen me and fourteen black and white cows downstream having a drink so I knew I'd have to go straight across. But I didn't know whose side the river was on, it might help me swim or it might drown me.

The theme of warfare between men and animals is drawn directly from the Bible:

> And I looked, and behold a pale horse: and his name that sat on him was Death, and Hell followed with him. And power was given unto them over the fourth part of the earth, to kill with sword, and with hunger, and with death, and with the beasts of the earth (Revelation 8:6, King James Version).

The very last lines of the play tie in with the theme of apocalyptic mythology and much else. When Joan steps into the river, Churchill is recalling a whole raft of mythology, from Jesus's baptism in the river Jordan to the river of forgetfulness that, in Greek myth, the dead must cross to enter the underworld:

> I knew it was my only way of getting here so at last I put one foot in the river. It was very cold but so far that was all. When you've just stepped in

> you can't tell what's going to happen.
> The water laps around your ankles in
> any case.

This relates to the afterlife, referred to in the play's title as a place far away. In the declaration "you can't tell what's going to happen," Churchill is denying the whole of prophecy that the apocalypse depends on, but even that is no more than a symbol for her denial of literature. The play ends in nonsense because Churchill has a sense that literature, or at least the possibility of communicating genuine meaning through literature, has ended.

Romantic Love

In *Reflections on "The Name of the Rose,"* novelist Umberto Eco offers the opinion that a self-reflective character cannot tell someone he loves that he loves her madly because the words that he might use have been used in romance novels and become ridiculous. But such a character could avoid the debasement of his feelings through cliché by telling his beloved that he loves her madly, just like a character in a romance novel. This is a classic postmodern analysis: one that references its own genre.

Eco is pointing out the absurdity that is part of the postmodern condition, but in *Far Away*, Churchill goes one step further. She constructs a romance in the play between Joan and Todd by dropping hints here and there in their dialogue throughout the second act. Todd starts to court Joan by inviting her out to eat and saying he wishes she would drop by his apartment. He compliments her work with praise that is obviously flattery. Joan gradually begins to return his interest, praising his judgment and seniority, and she defers to his opinions. He says that the only drawback to potentially losing his job would be that he would miss her—but in that case, she responds, she would quit. By the end of the act, when they are bickering who will let the other use some beads that they both want for their work, the audience is in no doubt about their feelings, and indeed in the third act, they are a couple. The whole thing proceeds with far more subtlety than a romance novel, but no one could mistake it for a genuine depiction of love either. Churchill is telling the audience: *romance between the two main characters is the most common device to drive a plot forward; I am showing you the conventional signs of romance, and you will read them*. Churchill does not need to show her audience reality. For her, all literature is clichéd, so a sort of summary of it is all that is required. She is pointing out that the entire idea of the romance plot is absurd.

Style

Postmodernism

Modernism was a literary and artistic movement of the late nineteenth and early twentieth centuries. It looked to the new world created by the industrial revolution as one of boundless possibility, advancing toward prosperity and order at a rapid, unstoppable rate. Modernist literature is confident about the future, about science and industry constantly making the world better, creating more wealth, more equality, and more freedom. The optimism of modernity met deep challenges in the crises of the twentieth century. The forces that had seemed to drive civilization forward came to endanger civilization in the two world wars, the failure of capitalism in the Great Depression, the failure of Communism in the Stalinist purges, the failure of science and industry in the environmental degradation produced by modern society, and the failure of all the systems working together in producing nuclear weapons and the Cold War. The human race and all life on earth seemed on the verge of extinction. The old confidence and faith in progress were shattered.

Postmodern art, especially after World War II, reacted to the collapse, not of civilization, but of confidence in civilization. Painting and sculpture used became more abstract, exploding viewers' perception of the world, and literature moved away from forms like rhyme and meter in poetry and traditional formats of the novel. While late modernist writers like T. S. Eliot (writing between the world wars) felt devastated by the breakdown of modernity, the typical response of a postmodernist writer is to view the broken landscape of the world comically, almost as a playground. Churchill's postmodern outlook is reflected in her view of society and government as inherently oppressive. *Far Away* is, on the one hand, set in modern Britain, but on the other in an oppressive state that can be compared to Stalin's Soviet Union or George Orwell's fictional Oceania in his novel *Nineteen Eighty-Four*. The message is that British society—one of the most liberal in the world—is oppressive and its citizens simply do not realize it. If Churchill were pressed to explain her work, she might say that the violence and tyranny of the parade stand for the human suffering caused by the poverty and social inequality that persists in even the most advanced Western countries, whether in spite of or because of government polices and interventions. The absurdist or comic element of her work is revealed in the ridiculous hats that become the symbol of totalitarianism.

Theater of the Absurd

The theater of the absurd has developed since the 1950s out of the existentialist literature of Albert Camus and is seen in the work of British dramatists such as Samuel Beckett, Harold Pinter, and Tom

Stoppard. It is one of the main forms of modernist drama. Its main idea is that human life and art have no meaning, and the attempt to communicate through the drama itself is broken down as the irrational nature of existence is exposed by the play. Absurdism leads to an inability to communicate, ending not in a dramatic climax but in silence. Churchill takes the ideas of the theater of the absurd almost as her script for *Far Away*. Katherine Tozer (who played the adult Joan in the original production) recalls the rehearsal process of *Far Away* in a reminiscence written for Philip Roberts's *About Churchill:*

> I had stopped saying the last line —"The water laps around your ankles in any case"—like it was the last line and we had a major breakthrough. The play just needed to be left hanging there, and the great heavy front cloth [curtain] bashed into the stage with an amplified thud like the building was falling down and the theatre had been broken.

The play builds up to fantastic pitch of absurd rejection of reality and then simply ends, falling silent with no possible resolution.

Historical Context

Public Executions

In all Western countries, executions of criminals were public affairs viewed by large crowds until late in the nineteenth century. Think of all the cowboy films that show public hangings in the Old West. Executions in Victorian London were festivities attended by thousands of people, with vendors and entertainers catering to the crowds. Public executions were justified on the grounds that because so few criminals were caught and punished, it was the only way to keep the fear of punishment in the public consciousness.

But the executions as practiced in *Far Away* go far beyond this. It is evident from the work pace kept up by Todd and Joan that they must make the hats for several parades a year, and there are other workshops besides theirs that they compete against for prizes. Todd also mentions at one point that there are other parades in which hats are not used but which are marked by some other similar special features. So Churchill is envisioning a version of British society in which no fewer than several thousand people are publicly executed on nationwide television every year. This level of mayhem can only be part of an apparatus of state terror. The goal is not to control crime but to stifle political dissent. The real-world counterparts that come to mind are the show trials in Soviet Russia in the 1930s, in which thousands of innocent people were convicted and executed on false charges of treason and counter-revolution. The executions themselves in that case were not public, but the trials were filmed and shown as newsreels. The same means of social control today is used by the Islamic Revolutionary government of Iran, albeit on a smaller scale.

As odd as it seems, the use of special costumes like Churchill's hats for criminals being executed also have historical precedent. They are part of a strategy to humiliate the condemned and make them seem different, so that the audience can be convinced to fear and hate them, never identify with them. The audience supports the executioners rather than their victims. In the Roman Empire, condemned criminals were often executed during the public games held in the Coliseum at Rome and in smaller amphitheaters throughout the Empire. During the lunch hour when there was a lull in the schedule of gladiatorial combats and wild beast hunts, the theater floor would be used for executions. Often, to increase the spectacle, they were dressed in costumes depicting mythic characters, and the manner of their execution sometimes re-enacted scenes from mythology (such as the legendary traitor Tarpeia being flung from a cliff). When Christians were executed, they were sometimes humiliated by being forcibly dressed in costumes representing the pagan gods. During the counter-reformation in the sixteenth and seventh and seventeenth, the Spanish Inquisition would organize mass executions of dozens of heretics at a time in a spectacle they called an *auto de fe*, or act of faith, considering that the executions would be an expression of public virtue. In that case, the victims were dressed in elaborate silk gowns with masks and pointed hats.

Critical Overview

Although *Far Away* has developed a favorable reputation among scholars and has been frequently revived, its initial reception was not completely enthusiastic. Reviewing the original production in 2000 in the *Guardian*, Michael Billington found that "although this 50-minute play about a descent into the dark ages' shocks and surprises, it moves from the real to the surreal in ways I found less than convincing." His dissatisfaction stemmed from the rapid pace of the play's development. The play moves from realism into "cosmic chaos" in a way that is impressive but "too swift to be dramatically convincing." He felt the viewer is forced to believe Churchill's argument rather than be persuaded, commenting: "while I am prepared to accept Churchill's thesis that we are slowly sliding into barbarism, I would prefer the case to be argued rather than presented as a dramatic given."

Ann Wilson, in her article "Hauntings: Ghosts and the Limits of Realism in *Cloud Nine* and *Fen* by Caryl Churchill," says that Churchill uses a "stunning theatricality … to critique social relations." That is, she uses the conventions and expectations of theater to make the audience think about elements of politics, economic life, and other important social issues. Churchill herself, though, seems to give much of the credit to the way the plays are staged by the Royal Court Theatre.

Unusually for a living author, Churchill is the subject of a volume in the Cambridge Companion series. Writing in this series, Dan Rebellato, in "On Churchill's Influences," judges that *"Far Away* ... has a claim to being the most influential play of the 2000s." In the same volume, Elin Diamond's essay "On Churchill and Terror" considers *Far Away* in connection with the ancient Roman play *Thyestes*, by Seneca, in which power and horror are seen as opposite to ordinary life; in *Far Away*, though, power and horror become part of the characters' everyday lives. Diamond finds, however, that the ending of *Far Away* nevertheless offers hope to its characters. Any serious analysis of *Far Away* sees it as a socialist allegory criticizing the British government. Siân Adiseshiah, in her 2009 book *Churchill's Socialism: Political Resistance in the Plays of Caryl Churchill*, argues that the general consensus that Churchill is a feminist playwright is at best a partial picture of her work; instead, she finds the origin of Churchill's thought in classic socialism, which Adiseshiah feels is too often shifted into the background in discussions of Churchill. She views *Far Away* as a reaction to the NATO interventions in the former Yugoslavia and Kuwait in the 1990s, which Churchill viewed as thoroughly imperialist.

What Do I Read Next?

- *The Blind Owl* (1937, translated into English in 1958) is a novel by the Iranian writer Sadegh Hedayat. It uses the imagery and techniques of surrealism in an attempt to break through to a deeper understanding of the meaning of existence.

- *A Kestrel for a Knave* (1973) is a classic young-adult novel by Barry Hines. It tells the story of a working-class boy from the north of England who is alienated from the oppressive environments of his family and school. The only thing that holds any meaning for him is a kestrel (a type of falcon) that he raised from a chick and taught to hunt. He finds new meaning in life through his connection with the natural world. It offers an alternative to the bleak view of humanity at war with nature in *Far Away*.

- *Caryl Churchill: A Casebook*, edited by Phyllis R. Randall and published in 1988, offers an early assessment of Churchill's life and work through a collection of scholarly articles.

- The fourth and most recent volume of Churchill's collected works, Plays: 4, was published in 2009. It contains a selection of her recent work, including *Cloud Nine, Bliss, Hotel, This Is a Chair, Blue Heart, A Number, Drunk Enough to Say I Love You?*, and her translation of August Strindberg's A *Dream Play*.

- Elaine Aston's 2010 *Caryl Churchill* offers a biography of Churchill and critical readings and commentaries on the most important of her plays.

- *Theatres of the Left, 1880-1935: Worker's Theatre Movements in Britain and America*, written by Raphael Samuel, Ewan MacColl, and Stuart Congrove and published in 1985, provides a history of the early Marxist drama that forms the historical background for the socialist themes in Churchill's work.

Sources

Adiseshiah, Siân, *Churchill's Socialism: Political Resistance in the Plays of Caryl Churchill,* Cambridge Scholars Press, 2009, pp. 195–218.

Artaud, Antonin, "The Theatre of Cruelty," in *The Theater and Its Double,* translated by Mary Caroline Richards, Grove Press, 1994, pp. 89–100.

Billington, Michael, "Surreal Shocks from CarylChurchill," in *Guardian,* December 1, 2000.

Brecht, Bertolt, *Brecht on Theatre: The Development of an Aesthetic,* edited and translated by John Willett, Hill and Wang, 1964, pp. 22–24, 179–205.

Churchill, Caryl, *Far Away,* Nick Hern, 2000.

Diamond, Elin, "On Churchill and Terror," in *The Cambridge Companion to Caryl Churchill,* edited by Elaine Aston and Elin Diamond, Cambridge University Press, 2009, pp. 125–43.

Eco, Umberto, *Reflections on "The Name of the Rose,"* Secker & Warburg, 1985, p. 67.

Esslin, Martin, *Theater of the Absurd,* 3rd ed., Vintage, 2004, pp. 15–28.

Orwell, George, *Nineteen Eighty-Four,* Harcourt Brace, 1949, pp. 246–73.

Rebellato, Dan, "On Churchill's Influences," in *The Cambridge Companion to Caryl Churchill,* edited by Elaine Aston and Elin Diamond, Cambridge University Press, 2009, pp. 163–79.

Richter, Hans, *Dada: Art and Anti-Art,* Thames & Hudson, 1997, p. 194.

Roberts, Philip, *About Churchill: The Playwright and the Work,* Faber and Faber, 2008, pp. xv–xxi, 145–50, 257–61.

Sophocles, "Oedipus the King," in *The Complete Greek Tragedies, Sophocles I,* translated by David Greene, University of Chicago Press, 1954, pp. 9–76.

Wilson, Ann, "Haunting: Ghosts and the Limits of Realism in *Cloud Nine* and *Fen* by Caryl Churchill," in *Drama on Drama: Dimensions of Theatricality on the Contemporary British Stage,* edited by Nicole Boireau, MacMillan, 1997, pp. 152–67.

Further Reading

Churchill, Caryl, *Top Girls,* Methuen, 1982.

> *Top Girls* is a study of the role and failures of feminism in Britain during its first few years under the influential prime minister Margaret Thatcher. It is probably Churchill's most influential play and is generally credited with forming the shape of modern British theater.

Cousin, Geraldine, *Churchill the Playwright,* Heinemann, 1989.

> A volume in the Methuen Theatre Profiles Series, this work provides an introduction to Churchill's life and her early work.

Lynn, Jonathan, and Anthony Jay, *Yes Prime Minister: The Diaries of the Right Hon. James Hacker,* Vol. 2, Guild, 1987.

> Adapted from the BBC television series *Yes Prime Minister,* this volume is a highly realistic (as opposed to surreal) satire of the British political system. The chapter "The Patron of the Arts" deals with the relationship between the government and the arts community; it notes the paradox of the

government having to pay through arts grants to support playwrights who do nothing but criticize the government. Although she is not named, Churchill is partly the target of the satire. The book as a whole gives insight into the political realities that Churchill is satirizing in an entirely different manner in *Far Away*.

Orwell, George, *Animal Farm: A Fairy Story,* Secker and Warburg, 1945.

> Orwell criticizes the history of the Russian revolution through allegory. He sets his story on an English farm on which the animals revolt, drive the farmer off his land, and begin to work the farm for themselves. The various historical figures of the revolution, such as Vladimir Lenin, Leon Trotsky, and Joseph Stalin are represented as pigs and other domestic animals.

Suggested Search Terms

Caryl Churchill

Far Away AND Churchill

theater of the absurd

theater of cruelty

surrealism

allegory

socialism AND theater

Thyestes

Printed in the USA
CPSIA information can be obtained
at www.ICGtesting.com
LVHW020550041023
760009LV00004B/622

9 781375 379823